CULTURE

in Papua New Guinea

Melanie Guile

Heinemann
LIBRARY

H www.heinemann.co.uk/library

Visit our website to find out more information about Heinemann Library books.

To order:

☎ Phone 44 (0) 1865 888066

🗎 Send a fax to 44 (0) 1865 314091

💻 Visit the Heinemann Bookshop at www.heinemann.co.uk/library to browse our catalogue and order online.

First published 2003 in Australia by Heinemann Library a division of Harcourt Education Australia, 18–22 Salmon Street, Port Melbourne Victoria 3207 Australia (a division of Reed International Books Australia Pty Ltd, ABN 70 001 002 357).

Series cover and text design by Stella Vassiliou
Paged by Stella Vassiliou
Edited by Carmel Heron
Production by Michelle Sweeney

Pre-press by Digital Imaging Group (DIG), Melbourne, Australia
Printed and bound in China by WKT Company Ltd.

ISBN 1 74070 063 5 (hardback)
07 06 05 04 03 02
10 9 8 7 6 5 4 3 2 1

ISBN 0 431 18127 6 (paperback)
09 08 07 06 05
10 9 8 7 6 5 4 3 2 1

British Library Cataloguing in Publication Data

Guile, Melanie.
Culture in Papua New Guinea.
306'.09953
A full catalogue record for this book is available from the British library.

Acknowledgements

Cover photograph of the mudmen of Asaro supplied by Australian Picture Library.

Other photographs supplied by: Alex Steffe/ Lochman Transparencies: pp. 7, 18, 26; All Australian Nature & General: pp. 10, 11, 16, 17, 28; Australian Picture Library: pp. 9, 13, 19, 20, 21, 23, 25, 27; Fred Adler: p. 14; Jean Paul Ferrero/AUSCAPE: p. 24; Mathias Kauage, *Barrasut Man (Parachute jumper)*, 1977, National Gallery of Australia, Canberra, Gordon Darling Fund 1990: p. 29; PhotoDisc: p. 6.

Every attempt has been made to trace and acknowledge copyright. Where an attempt has been unsuccessful, the publisher would be pleased to hear from the copyright owner so any omission or error can be rectified in subsequnt printings.

CONTENTS

Words that appear in bold, **like this**, are explained in the glossary on page 30.

CULTURE IN
Papua New Guinea

Sleeping dragon

Some say the people of Papua New Guinea (PNG) came from east Asia around 50 000 years ago. The earliest arrivals moved to land further up the river valleys as later tribes invaded the coast.

For thousands of years these separate tribal groups lived locked away from each other and the outside world. They had no metals, but worked in stone, bone and wood. There was no writing, but stories of the **ancestors** were told in chants and songs passed down through generations. Away from the coasts, trading did not exist and nature supplied the tribes with all they needed. The people believed that spirits and magical powers provided these things and had to be worshipped with complex **rituals**. The wheel was unknown, so travel was hard. Many mountain tribes had not been beyond their valley boundaries for centuries. Under these conditions, an astonishingly rich and varied culture thrived. Like a sleeping dragon, the country is only now stirring from its centuries-old slumber.

What is culture?

Culture is a people's way of living. It is the way people identify themselves as a group, separate and different from any other. Culture includes a group's language, social customs and habits, as well as its traditions of art, craft, dance, music and spiritual beliefs.

In the past, Papua New Guineans were generally **inward-looking** people. Small tribes lived isolated from one another in **inaccessible** valleys, coastal swamps or lonely islands. Neighbouring **clans** usually spoke different languages and viewed each other as enemies. Wars and **cannibalism** were common. This meant that each clan's world was small, self-sufficient and unchanging. In these conditions, thousands of unique cultures developed side by side with very little contact between them.

National flag of Papua New Guinea

The bird of paradise is sacred in many parts of the country. It represents the free spirit of the people. The stars of the Southern Cross show the country's links with other Pacific countries, including Australia.

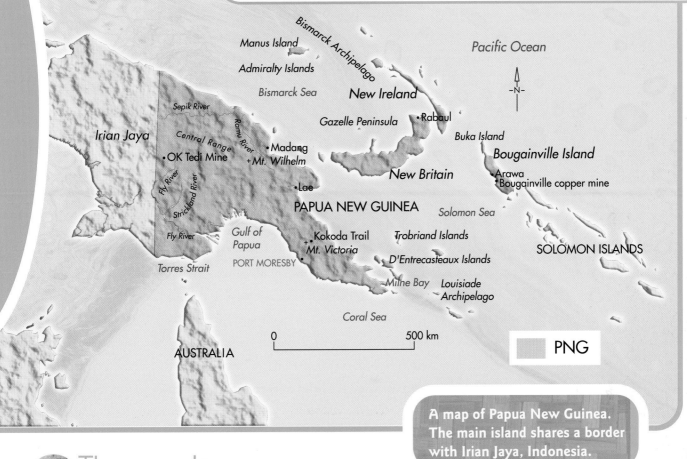

A map of Papua New Guinea. The main island shares a border with Irian Jaya, Indonesia.

The people

PNG is the most **diverse** culture in the world. In 2000, its population was estimated at 4 926 984, made up of over 1000 tribal groups speaking over 800 different languages – over one third of all the languages in the world. There are four main **ethnic** groups: the New Guineans in the north, the Papuans in the south, Highlanders in the mountainous inland valleys, and seafaring peoples around the coasts and offshore islands. Around 85 per cent of people live in rural villages and survive on an average income of $A5 a day.

Common traditions

In spite of the great diversity of the peoples of PNG, many similar cultural traditions are found throughout the country. The kinship (*wantok*) system offers some social security in a country that is too poor for pensions. The 'payback' revenge system means everyone is clear about the consequences of doing harm to another. The natural world is alive with the spirits of ancestors who are believed to bring luck or harm. Keeping them content is an important part of everyday life throughout PNG. Across the country, community ties are very strong. Boys and girls are taught the duties and privileges of adulthood in **initiation** ceremonies, and know their place in the clan. This rich sense of community is the strength of PNG culture, but it does not cope well with change. Once away from their villages, men and women often question traditional values and lose their sense of belonging.

Spiritual life

Almost every aspect of PNG culture is linked with spiritual beliefs. Beautifully carved ancestor spirit figures stare from the roof pole of the *haus tambaran* (spirit house) to give protection to the inhabitants. **Asmat** shields from the Papuan Gulf express the soul of the warrior and make him unbeatable in battle. During initiation ceremonies in the Sepik River district, elders take on the spiritual power of the clan's ancestors by speaking the sacred names. In the North Solomon islands, men blow flutes to summon friendly spirits to important village events including births, marriages, wars, harvests and deaths.

Spiritual beliefs in PNG culture are commonly expressed in dance.

The *bigman* (chief) holds village ceremonies in the *haus tambaran* (spirit house).

Life in the towns

Port Moresby is the capital of PNG and the seat of government. It is an unsettled and edgy place to live. Huge Mercedes cars display the status of the politicians inside. Wealthy citizens build high fences around their houses to keep out criminal 'rascal' gangs that roam the streets after dark. Armed security guards and razor wire surround hotels, and foreigners are often targets of violent crime. Large **shanty towns,** on the outskirts of the city, house unemployed **drifters** from the country who are the cause of much of the street crime. The town of Lae also has a reputation as a dangerous place – especially for women. In efforts to improve the situation in cities, **curfews** and bans on street gangs and alcohol have been tried. But the problems of unemployment, poverty and the clash of modern and traditional cultures are deep rooted and hard to solve.

Media

In Papua New Guinea there are two English language daily newspapers, and weekly papers in **pidgin** and English. Radios are hugely popular and the National Broadcasting Corporation has two networks. NAU-FM is a private radio station operating in Port Moresby. EM.TV is the only television station in the country, and music-video shows are very popular.

Dance, music and drama are woven together in village rituals to celebrate or mourn, or please the ancestral spirits. Over 85 per cent of Papua New Guineans still live traditional lives, and the old dances and songs form a vital part of their culture. However, time has not stood still in PNG and modern music thrives, particularly in the towns and offshore islands. Rabaul, in the New Britain **archipelago,** was famous as a centre of local pop and rock music before it was smothered in volcanic ash. Now studios in Port Moresby produce recordings of local performers, and PNG music is popular all over the Pacific.

Dance

There is an old saying in Papua – 'We don't dance for no meaning'. Every tribal group has its own dances that accompany important festivals, social events and spiritual rituals. Dances are held on special occasions such as weddings, funerals, initiation ceremonies and **yam** harvests. Many songs and dances are based on spiritual beliefs about the ancestors of the village, and costumes represent aspects of them.

In most parts of PNG, dancing sessions go on for many days and nights – sometimes up to six weeks. Ground in the village is cleared and swept, and **rattan** mats are placed around the edge. In Oro Province in north-east PNG, the Maisin people begin dancing sessions with a mock duel. The best drummers in the village take up the beat and the women arrive beating pots and pans and shouting to try to distract them. The men win and, with much laughter, the women retreat.

Dances consist of foot and body movements and are usually danced in sets with short breaks for rests in between. Songs and chants usually accompany dances in PNG and the men and women generally dance together. Some of the words to the songs are so ancient that the meanings have been long forgotten.

Playing with fire

At the Goroka cultural festival, Highland women dance with cups of fire on their heads. These are fed with small twigs and leaves by other dancers to keep the fires going.

Mudmen of Asaro

The Asaro tribe imitate dead people in their dances. Their looming, ghostly costumes are enough to terrify any enemy. They wear huge, ash-white clay masks with hollow, skull-like faces, and smear thick white clay over their bodies to imitate the bloodless skin of corpses. They dance slowly, bent over, and flick themselves with twig fly swatters to repel the imaginary flies attracted to the dead flesh! The mudmen of Asaro are an eerie sight among the riot of colour of the other Highland tribes at cultural festivals *(sing-sings)*.

The half-man bush spirit

A Highland myth is celebrated in the dance of the half-man spirit. Men painted half-black, half-white, with long claws on one hand, mimic this bush spirit who, they believe, has only half a body. He lives in the jungle with his half-wife and children. Villagers say they know where he has been by the single footprints he leaves behind.

Dancing costumes

Tribes along the Middle Sepik River make elaborate masked costumes (*tumbuan*) for ceremonial dances. The men smear mud over turtle or coconut shells to form the masks, then paint them with coloured clay or charcoal. The masks are decorated with shells, pig tusks and **cassowary** feathers. They do not have eyeholes because they are not worn on the face but lashed to a cone-shaped frame. This is covered with flowers, leaves and a **raffia** skirt at the base. The dancer gets inside the frame, with the mask attached, and moves it to the beat of the dance.

Every tribal group in PNG has its own dances to accompany important events.

Traditional music

Drums, flutes and wooden horns are used in traditional rituals all over PNG. In Tangu, in the Madang district, gongs are used to announce community events. Everyone in the village has their own gong signal, and important information is communicated through these percussion instruments. Eastern Highland men blow flutes as a symbol of male power, and to call up spirits. The Gimi people of Labogai district play flutes at boys' initiations and pig festivals. Women are not permitted to see these sacred instruments.

Flutes are sacred instruments used to call up spirits at initiations and festivals.

Modern music

PNG has some of the most popular bands in the Pacific. PNG pop music is a mix of **indigenous** rhythms and reggae sounds with a pop–rock edge. It is a rough sound with lots of percussion and electric guitar. Lyrics are in pidgin or English and have themes like love, religion and growing up. String bands are hugely popular throughout the Pacific region and the best come from PNG. Based on acoustic guitars and ukuleles with added electric instruments, string bands have an islander sound with a hint of country music. The most famous string band was the now disbanded Moab Stringband fronted by the hugely popular singer–songwriter George Telek.

There is a thriving music industry in PNG. Before a volcanic eruption wiped it out in 1994, Rabaul was home to famous recording studios Pacific Gold and CHM. Now based in Port Moresby, local recording companies produce over 90 per cent of the music recordings played in the country. They also produce their own video clips, which are featured on EM.TV, the only PNG television channel.

MYTHS,
traditions and customs

Ancient and modern

PNG is a tribal culture. Around 85 per cent of the people still live traditional lives, farming and hunting for food and maintaining the spiritual beliefs and customs of their ancestors. Although 97 per cent of the population is Christian and every village has its own church and pastor, the ancient tribal myths and rituals survive alongside this faith. Keeping ancestor spirits happy is vital to the wellbeing of a village. Any sickness or bad luck means an evil influence is about – perhaps witchcraft or **sorcery** – and spiritual healers are as important as doctors.

Strong cultural beliefs have helped keep communities together, but now these ties are loosening. The influence of western goods and values is undermining young people's sense of belonging. Unemployment has led many young men to migrate to cities like Lae and Port Moresby for work. There, they live in squalid shanty towns with no support from village elders, competing for the few jobs available.

Power and status

Wealth and power have always been important in PNG culture. *Kina* shells are still worn by well-off tribespeople to show how rich they are. Highland *bigmen* (chiefs) show their status by giving extravagant gifts to friends and rivals at *moga* ceremonies – and expecting equally costly gifts or favours back. Valuable boar tusks are displayed on the house poles of the wealthiest families in the village, and *bigmen* will marry as many wives as they can afford.

Perhaps because of their traditional interest in material wealth, many Highland and Milne Bay tribes have adapted well to western material values. They are good business people, and keep a shrewd eye on the tourist dollar. Handcrafts made for the tourist trade have brought much-wanted cash to many remote communities, which depend on this income to improve their lifestyles.

Wantok

Wantok is pidgin for 'one talk', or people who speak the same language. *Wantoks* are members of the same clan and must be loyal to one another. The positive side of this means that there are strong family ties – food, houses and jobs are shared, and members of the clan help each other out. However, the system also lends itself to **corruption**. Powerful *bigmen* favour their *wantoks* in distributing wealth, and politicians are more likely to give the best jobs and salaries to their *wantoks*. Even the courts can be corrupted, and judges sometimes let their *wantoks* off lightly.

Well-off tribespeople wear *kina* shells around their necks to show their wealth.

Malangan funeral rites

The Malangan people of remote New Ireland carve life-sized figures of the dead as part of their funeral ceremonies. Depending on the clan, bodies may be buried, burned or set adrift in a boat. The dead person's soul crosses to the ancestors' world with the help of nature spirits, and the carved image is displayed at the funeral feast.

13

The payback system

For thousands of years, the payback system has been a way of life for most tribal people in PNG. Payback means that any injury, death or harm caused must be revenged in the same manner. This applies even if the harm is suspected rather than real, or is caused by an accident. Feuds between tribes can last for years and cost many lives, although mass killings are very rare. Police are often unable to stop clansmen taking their revenge, and tribal loyalties often cause them to turn a blind eye. Tourists travelling on the Highland Highway, where payback is still very strong, are advised never to stop on site if they run over a pedestrian or a valuable pig, but to drive to the nearest police station. Today, money is often acceptable as a peace offering, but payback violence is still common outside the larger towns.

Human prizes

Fifty years ago, many tribal people in the main island of PNG were cannibals and head hunters. Young Highland warriors set out in raiding parties to neighbouring clans to capture heads, which would be smoked over a fire to preserve them, or hung up on skull racks in the men's houses. It was believed that these heads contained powerful magic, and brought protection from evil to those in the village. Sometimes the bodies of dead family members would be eaten as a sign of love and respect, and the bones preserved for luck.

Traditionally, hunted heads were thought to contain powerful magic and bring protection from evil.

Even today, Highland people wear relatives' bones as part of their traditional dress to keep the spirits of loved ones near them. Although headhunting is outlawed, travellers in the Western Highlands have occasionally disappeared, and some say their bodies were found without the heads.

Boys' initiations are elaborate rituals that involve some sort of ordeal or task that must be completed.

Growing up

In traditional PNG culture, there is no such thing as adolescence. Young teenagers are regarded as children until they complete their initiation (coming of age) rituals. Boys' initiations are taken very seriously, and involve very elaborate rituals. These vary from region to region, but all involve some sort of ordeal or task that boys must complete, like spending weeks in the jungle alone, or planting their first yam field.

In the Sepik River district, initiation lasts a month. Boys undergo a one-hour ceremony in which their bodies are cut with a bamboo blade to create hundreds of small scars. These represent the scales of the crocodile, the tribe's **totem**, which enters the boys' souls to guide them through life. When the initiation is complete, the boys emerge as men and are given adult duties and responsibilities.

Sky world myths

Many tribal groups in PNG believe there is a sky world above, just like this one. The inland Ayon people tell how a sky man, Tumbrenjak, climbed down to Earth to hunt and could not get back because the rope ladder was cut. He became the father of all human beings on Earth. The Keraki Papuans on the south-west coast believe that when it rains hard the sky beings are angry. They look up anxiously in case the rattan floor of the sky world collapses with the weight of the excess water.

15

COSTUME

Living art

Like every aspect of life in PNG, the art of traditional dress and self-decoration expresses important aspects of a person's identity and tribal community. The colours and designs of the face paint, the tattoos, the kind of bird feathers worn in the headdress – all have stories to tell about the person's tribe and home district, their wealth and status in the village, and so on. For this reason, body decoration is highly developed in PNG, especially in the Highlands where traditional culture remains very strong.

For *sing-sings*, tribal groups spend hours preparing spectacular costumes, body ornaments and headpieces.

Tribal dress

There are three main parts to each costume: the headdress, face and body painting, and ornaments. Wigs are made of human hair or plant fibre and decorated with flowers, leaves and feathers. The colours and patterns of the face paint indicate the wearer's tribe and status. Pearl shells, tusks and strings of dogs' teeth are used as jewellery, and show the person's wealth. Headbands of blue-green beetles are often worn and possum-fur capes are draped around the neck. Both men and women dress in this way for important ceremonies, but males wear more richly decorated costumes.

Each tribe has its own distinctive costume. Huli men from the Southern Highlands are famous for their elaborate and beautiful wigs. Young men dressed for the bachelor dance wear yellow, red and blue face paint, and a large wig of human hair decorated with parrot and bird of paradise feathers.

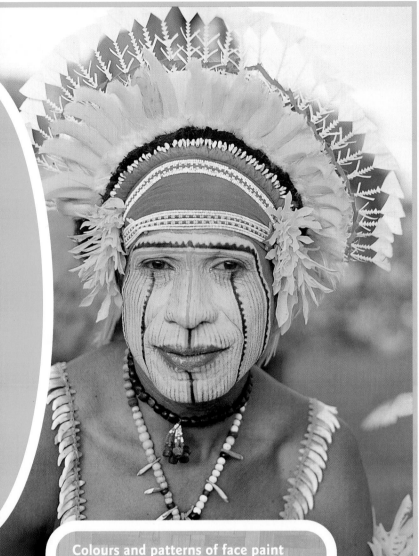

Colours and patterns of face paint indicate the wearer's tribe and status.

Face paint

Face and body painting is traditional in the Highlands. Natural materials are still used to make the colours, including charcoal, powdered white shells, vegetable dyes and yellow, red and white clays. The skin is oiled first to make a good base, and the **pigment** is put on with a brush made from the chewed end of a stick. It can take many hours to paint the complex designs, and the whole family helps out. For important events like the Highland *sing-sings*, manufactured paints are often used because they are easy to use and have a wider colour range. White correction fluid is becoming popular, but the brush does not give as fine a line as the traditional twig!

Not long ago, the Huli were feared cannibals in the Tari Highlands. Young men would be sent alone into the jungle to learn bush skills and prepare for manhood. They would begin to grow their hair in preparation for making their first wig, which was a symbol of their coming of age as warriors ready for war.

Modern dress

When they are not in costume for traditional celebrations, almost everyone in PNG wears second-hand western clothes, often from Australia. Travelling merchants buy these old clothes in bulk very cheaply – $A10 for a 50-kilogram bag of 'mixed shirts' – and sell them in the villages.

Men's wear

Traditionally, Highland men wore no clothes except for a woven plant-fibre belt and penis **sheath** made from the hardened skin of a kind of vegetable marrow. Penis gourds are still worn on ceremonial occasions and are highly prized by tourists as souvenirs. Many young men in the towns admire the American Rambo style and often wear denim jackets and red **bandanas** around their foreheads. T-shirts printed with religious **slogans** are also popular.

Jewellery

Bilas (jewellery) is a pidgin word meaning 'flash'. Wearing costly ornaments has always been an important way of showing a family's wealth and status in PNG, and it still is. Before Europeans came to the main island, shells were used as a form of money. Gold-lipped pearl shells were carved into curved shapes called *kina* and traded for valuable goods. Circles of smaller shells called *toea* were like coins and were often worn through the nose or as necklaces. These words survive today: in PNG's paper currency, 100 *toea* coins equal 1 *kina*, and real shells are often used as money in ceremonies such as weddings.

Every body ornament has meaning. Strings of dog, pig, porpoise or fruit–bat teeth indicate a person's wealth. *Bigmen* (village chiefs) wear *kina* around their necks to show their status and power. Human bones are sometimes worn, either as necklaces and bracelets or through the nose. These may be the bones of loved relatives who have died, as the power of their spirits is believed to linger in their remains. Although 97 per cent of the population of PNG is Christian, older beliefs like this remain strong throughout the country.

Shells are highly valued for traditional costumes

Tattoos

In Manus Island, off the south-east coast of the mainland, body tattoos are common. Once they were applied to both women and men by punching sharpened wood or bone needles and dye into the skin. It was a painful process, and only people of high status were permitted to have tattoos. Girls and women were tattooed at special stages of their lives, and to mark the safe return of a male relative from a sea voyage. Today you can still see full-body tattoos on older women, but felt pen is used as a painless and temporary alternative for special occasions.

Tattoos were traditionally applied by punching sharpened needles and dye into the skin. Today, felt pen or paint are used as painless alternatives for special occasions.

Sing-sing cultural festivals

For two days and nights in September, the sportsground at Goroka becomes a living sea of colour. Over 20 000 men and women gather in traditional costume to compete for cash prizes. So brilliant is the effect that tourists and photographers come from all over the world to enjoy the scene.

FOOD

Traditional food

The traditional staple foods in PNG – sweet potato (*kaukau*) and sago – are starchy and bland. They fill empty stomachs quickly but are not very nourishing. Sweet potatoes were brought to PNG long ago by Spanish traders from South America. Most meals are made from fresh ingredients available locally, including vegetables from village gardens, fruits like mango, banana and coconuts, and fish or possum, tree kangaroo and wild birds. Most village families own a pig or chickens, but these are regarded as a form of wealth and only eaten at special feasts (*mumu*) held for weddings or funerals. Today's villagers have access to tinned and dried western foods, but they are very expensive.

A Trobriand Island villager stacks yams in a village compound during a yam harvest festival

Yams

The root vegetable *kaukau* is a kind of potato, or yam, and is grown in village vegetable gardens throughout PNG, except in the lowlands. Growing yams is an important part of village life and good *kaukau* farmers are treated with great respect. Ceremonies and celebrations accompany the yam harvest, with a procession through the village to the yam house where the roots are stored. In the Highlands, yams form part of everyday meals. They are usually roasted in the fire or boiled, and can be served as a savoury meal with green vegetables from the women's plots or sweetened with sticks of sugar cane.

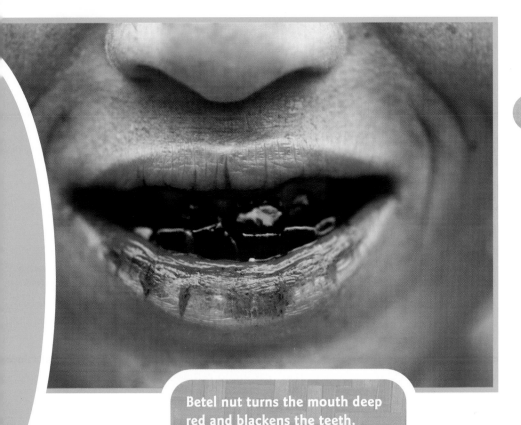

Betel nut turns the mouth deep red and blackens the teeth.

Sago

Sago is a food made from the soft bark of the sago palm tree. It is a native plant that grows in the lowlands where soils are too poor and swampy to grow yams. The women spend many hours stripping the bark, soaking it in water and beating it to remove the bitter taste. The pithy bark turns into a white flour that is cooked and eaten with vegetables. Coastal people eat a greater variety of food, including many different types of fish, lobsters and crabs. These are flavoured with coconut milk and spices like ginger and nutmeg, traded from nearby Indonesia.

Betel nut

Betel nut (*buai*) is the acorn-sized nut of a palm tree. The nut is peeled and chewed together with mustard stick and crushed coral powder. The effect is to create lots of saliva, and locals constantly eject streams of bright red **spittle**. Some city buildings – like airports and hospitals – have established 'no-spit' zones to combat the problem. *Buai* turns the mouth and tongue deep red and blackens the teeth, but it is popular throughout the country.

WOMEN AND GIRLS

Second best

It is not easy being a woman in PNG. Although all women are allowed to vote, and the country's laws make it illegal to favour males over females, women are treated as second best in almost every part of the country. In the past, tribal **taboos** and customs generally helped to protect women and girls from harm. Now traditions are breaking down, especially among the young men who leave the villages to seek work in towns. This has resulted in more family violence against women and girls in PNG.

Women's work

Women look after the house and children, cook all the meals, carry water and tend the vegetable gardens. Many women also produce craft works for sale in the market towns where tourists buy them for a few dollars. Cash like this is hard to come by in PNG, and can be used to buy luxuries like tinned food, imported fabric or western medicines. Wives are under the control of their husbands and eldest sons, and must do as they are told. A woman should not approach a man to talk to him, or eat at the same table – even with her husband and sons.

Marriage

Women are expected to marry young and have children straight away. When a girl reaches about 16 she is ready for marriage and must be bought with a 'bride price'. This is usually in the form of pigs or chickens, which are a form of wealth in PNG. The bride price is set by the girl's father, and is often very high. If a young man likes a girl he must find this price before he can marry, and it can take many years of working and saving. In some parts of the country, men have more than one wife, which can cause tension in the family.

Human currency

Young girls are sometimes offered as compensation in tribal disputes. In 1998, the Jimi clan in Western Highland Province offered two teenage girls as payment to settle a fight. Fortunately, the National Court ordered an inquiry and the girls were returned to their village.

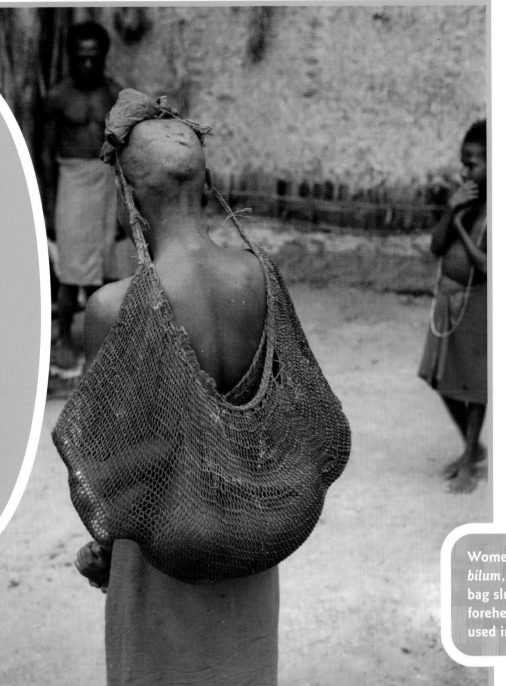

Women carry their babies in a *bilum*, which is a handmade string bag slung over the shoulder or forehead. Leaves, bark or rags are used in place of nappies.

Health

There is very little health care for women in PNG, so mothers and their babies often do not get the medical help they need. For this reason, many women die during childbirth, and an increasing number of newborn babies do not survive. Over 60 out of every 1000 children born in PNG do not live to their first birthday. One-third of babies who do survive do not get enough to eat. A small number of women's clinics are run by churches and aid organisations, but they reach only a tiny fraction of the women who need help. Unfortunately, the situation is getting worse, and women in PNG (on average) lived healthier, longer lives ten years ago than they do today.

A brighter picture

The picture of women's lives in PNG is not all negative. Sixty-three per cent of women in PNG can read and write. Although there are 15 per cent fewer girls in primary school than boys, the gap is narrowing. National laws protect women's rights, and courts often overturn unfair judgements against women given by local village councils. The **constitution** guarantees women equal property, marriage and family rights and there is a government Office of Women's Affairs in Port Moresby dedicated to improving women's place in PNG society. Some women hold senior posts in government, business and the professions.

At the village level, community life is strong and women do not struggle alone. Every woman looks out for the children and minds the old people or the sick, so the burden of domestic work is shared. Women and children share in village celebrations, dancing through the night beside the men. However, most musical instruments are *tabu* (forbidden) to women, who must not even look at a flute being played in case they keep away the spirits it is calling up.

In the Trobriand Islands, off the east coast of the mainland, the **Polynesian** culture is matrilineal, which means all property is passed on to the female side of the family. Male chiefs still control the islands, but the women's property rights mean they have some power and are treated with respect.

As well as looking after the house and children, this woman from the Sepik area makes traditional masks to sell to tourists.

There are fewer girls than boys in primary schools in PNG, but the gap is narrowing.

Women speaking out

In March 1999, after nine years of war, the women of Bougainville Island marched for peace and independence on International Women's Day. Over 700 women held a rally in the capital Arawa. Leaders from the local government and the Bougainville Women's Council urged the audience to remember their ancient traditional role as landowners on the island and called on the national government to recognise the right of the people of Bougainville to rule themselves.

Witch hunt

In the Eastern Highlands of PNG, bad luck, illness or sudden death are often blamed on *sangumas*, as witches are called. Women accused of witchcraft are sometimes injured or even killed by villagers, who believe they have called up evil spirits against them. Old or single women are the most likely to be accused.

ARTS AND CRAFTS

Art in life

Art is part of everyday life in Papua New Guinea. Carvings, decorations and paintings are made to express key aspects of the social and spiritual lives of the villagers. Beautiful carvings on house posts and **gables** represent spirit ancestors who guard the buildings. Brilliant colours painted on faces indicate the clan and status of the dancer. Ghostly masks and images painted on shields and weapons scare away enemies and give power to the owner. Although the artists and craftspeople who make these things are highly skilled and proud of their work, they see themselves as expressing the values and power of the community and the spirit world.

Carving a totem pole. Carvings express important aspects of the social and spiritual lives of villagers.

Masks

Traditional masks are made to represent ancestors and spirits and are used for important ceremonies. Those made without eyeholes are not worn but displayed on the prows of boats or in spirit houses called *haus tambaran*. These masks are carved from wood or made from turtle shells, and decorated with teeth, plant fibre and shells. Life-sized woven rattan figures called *tumbuan* represent the creation or clan spirit. Some are so sacred they are brought out only once a year at special rituals.

Savi (meaning 'power' or 'knowledge' in pidgin) are the most powerful masks. They draw the ancestor spirits and are displayed on house gables and on the speech-maker's stool in the *haus tambaran*. The tongue on a *savi* mask sticks out in a show of aggression. Only the *bigmen* (chiefs) may handle *savi* masks. *Mai* masks represent the teachers in boys' coming-of-age ceremonies. They are usually shown as pairs of brothers and sisters. The tribal elder wears a *mai* mask to take on the identity of the spirits who teach the youths. Masks are also worn as good luck charms, especially in hunting parties.

A Sepik painting on the gable of a *haus tambaran*

Skull racks

The skulls of relatives and enemies killed in battle were traditionally believed to contain powerful magic. They were decorated and displayed on finely carved skull racks in the men's house to bring courage and luck to the inhabitants. Skull racks were large human figures carved of wood then painted and decorated. The skulls were hung from them with grass string, or piled on a shelf in front. Although heads are no longer hunted and shown, the skull racks themselves, hoisted high in the men's houses, are still an awesome sight.

Spirit boards

Boards made of beaten bark were painted with protective spirits and hung from house gables and ceilings in men's and women's huts. These spirit or story boards were very important to the people of the Gulf of Papua because they kept away evil spirits and sickness. They were also used to tell the future and to predict the outcome of war. Now carved and painted on wood, not bark, they are produced in large numbers for the tourist trade, but remain excellent examples of fine Papua New Guinean art.

Crafts

Shining bowls in the shape of fish are typical of the fine crafts of the Trobriand Islanders. Known for their woodcarving throughout PNG, the islanders also make furniture in the shapes of animals and walking sticks for the tourist trade. Their carvings are often inlaid with mother of pearl and are greatly prized.

Traditional coil pots, made by moulding snakes of clay into vessels, are made by the people of Aibom on the Sepik River. Their pottery has distinctive face patterns on the sides, picked out in white lime to highlight the decoration.

Finely plaited and woven grass belts are a feature of traditional dress in the Highlands. Incredibly intricate designs are woven and knotted into these belts, which are often decorated with leaves and bark. Bougainville Island is the home of the famous *buka* basket weavers – the best in Papua New Guinea.

Weapons

Weapons were once sacred to the warriors who depended on them in battle. Daggers were made of bone or stone and sharpened to a fierce point. Swords were made with sharks' teeth embedded along the blade. Traditionally, the spirit in his shield protected the warrior in combat, so the making of a shield was a sacred act. The Asmat shield-makers of the Gulf of Papua are said to be the finest shield-makers in the world, and examples of their spectacular craftsmanship hang in galleries around the world.

A traditional axe, made from sharpened stone, wood and woven grass

A stencil by Mathias Kauage entitled *Barrasut Man (Parachute Jumper)*

Modern art

Not all of PNG's art is traditional. The few who are able to afford a university education can study painting at the University of Papua New Guinea in Port Moresby. A number of modern artists, such as Mathias Kauage and Gickmai Kundun, have gained international reputations and are shown in galleries overseas.

Sculptor Gickmai Kundun is one of the country's most respected modern artists. He prefers to work with 'found' scrap metal like rusty off-cuts and bumper bars from old car wrecks. His style is deliberately rough, unpolished and unfinished to show its handmade origins. Although Kundun often draws on traditional stories, he also expresses modern ideas in his sculptures. A work exhibited at the Port Moresby Art School in the 1990s was called *Nuclear Testing in the Pacific* and was intended as an environmental protest. Gickmai has won international awards for his artworks, which are beautifully textured, complex and pleasing to look at.

GLOSSARY

ancestors   forefathers; people from whom one is descended

archipelago   group of islands

Asmat   from the Asmat people of the south coast of Irian Jaya, whose artworks are popular with tourists and collectors

bandana   fabric band worn about the forehead

cannibalism   the practice of eating human flesh

cassowary   large running bird related to the ostrich

clan   family or tribal group

constitution   rules by which a state is governed

corruption   unethical or criminal activities by government officials or other powerful people

curfew   set time (usually at night) during which citizens must not be outdoors

diverse   mixed, made up of many different parts or types

drifters   homeless people; people who travel about aimlessly

ethnic   from a different culture or country

gable   triangular upper part of a wall at the end of a ridged roof

inaccessible   unable to be reached or travelled to

indigenous   native to a country or region

initiation   ceremony to mark an important stage in a person's life

inward-looking   concentrating on their own affairs, not those of others

pidgin   a simple language introduced by European traders to communicate with tribal groups

pigment   colouring material used as paint or dye

Polynesian   from the area that includes the Hawaiian Islands, Easter Island and the major island groups Samoa, Cook, Line, Tonga and French Polynesia

raffia   palm-leaf fibre used for making hats, baskets, skirts, etc.

rattan   the branches of climbing palms, which are used for wickerwork

rituals   traditional religious or spiritual ceremonies

shanty town   community of roughly built shacks, often on the outskirts of a city

sheath   close-fitting cover

slogan   short, catchy phrase or motto

sorcery   wizardry, enchantment

spittle   saliva or spit produced in the mouth

taboos   things that are forbidden or set apart as sacred

totem   an emblem of a clan, family or group

yam   root vegetable like a potato

FURTHER *information*

Book

Thompson, L. and S. Coate *Fighting for Survival* series – *The Trobriand Islanders of Papua New Guinea*. Reed Library. Cardigan Street, Melbourne, 1997.

Websites

Gickmai Kundun: www.abc.net.au/arts/artok/visual/s200701.htm

Mathias Kauage: www.abc.net.au/arts/artok/visual/s200716.htm

Art: www.art-pacific.com/artifacts/nuguinea/tocnugui.htm

Artifacts: www.mightymedia.com.au/tambaran/index.html

INDEX